ERNEST SHACKLETON
ANTARCTIC EXPLORER

Evelyn Dowdeswell, Julian Dowdeswell
and Angela Seddon

Raintree is an imprint of Capstone Global Library Limited, a company incorporated in England and Wales having its registered office at 7 Pilgrim Street, London, EC4V 6LB – Registered company number: 6695582

www.raintree.co.uk
myorders@raintreepublishers.co.uk

Text © Capstone Global Library Limited 2015
The moral rights of the proprietor have been asserted.

Edited by Clare Lewis
Designed by Richard Parker
Picture research by Tracy Cummins
Production by Helen McCreath
Originated by Capstone Global Library Ltd
Printed and bound in China

ISBN 978 1 406 28474 4
18 17 16 15 14
10 9 8 7 6 5 4 3 2 1

British Library Cataloguing in Publication Data
A full catalogue record for this book is available from the British Library.

Acknowledgements
We would like to thank the following for permission to reproduce photographs:
Julian Dowdeswell: 5, 28; Governors of Dulwich College: 7; Licensed with permission of the Scott Polar Research Institute, University of Cambridge: 4, 6 Right, 8, 9 Left, 9 Right, 10, 11, 12 Top, 12 Bottom, 13, 14, 15, 16, 17, 18, 19 Top, 19 Bottom Right, 20, 21 Right, 21 Left, 22, 23, 24 Bottom Right, 24 Top, 25, 26, 27 Right, 27 Left, 27 Middle, Cover; Seamus Taaffe with permission of Richard & Claudia Greene: 6 Left; Shutterstock: Aleksey Stemmer, Cover Background, Inside Design Element.

We would like to thank Lucy Martin and Bryan Lintott for their invaluable help in the preparation of this book.

Every effort has been made to contact copyright holders of material reproduced in this book. Any omissions will be rectified in subsequent printings if notice is given to the publisher.

All the internet addresses (URLs) given in this book were valid at the time of going to press. However, due to the dynamic nature of the internet, some addresses may have changed, or sites may have changed or ceased to exist since publication. While the author and publisher regret any inconvenience this may cause readers, no responsibility for any such changes can be accepted by either the author or the publisher.

Contents

Some words are shown in bold, **like this**. You can find out what they mean by looking in the glossary.

Who was Ernest Shackleton?

Ernest Shackleton was one of the greatest British polar explorers that ever lived. He travelled to **Antarctica** four times and faced many hardships there. He will always be remembered for his bravery and for saving the lives of his men.

Shackleton was a famous polar explorer.

Antarctica is the coldest continent on Earth. It is almost completely covered by ice.

Southern Ocean

Antarctica

Antarctica is the most southerly continent in the world. The land is covered in ice and snow. To get there, explorers had to cross the cold and stormy Southern Ocean by ship.

Growing up

Ernest Shackleton was born on 15 February 1874 in County Kildare in Ireland. When he was ten, his family moved to England. He had a happy childhood with his brother and eight sisters.

Ernest was taught at home in this big house in Ireland.

When Ernest was a boy, he liked reading poetry and adventure stories about the sea. He always wanted to become a sailor.

Shackleton's first trip to Antarctica

In 1901, Shackleton joined Captain Robert Falcon Scott on the ship *Discovery*. Scott was another famous polar explorer. They wanted to be the first people in the world to reach the **South Pole**, near the middle of **Antarctica**.

Discovery carried the men, dogs and supplies needed to live in Antarctica.

Scott, Shackleton and their friend, Edward Wilson, were the first people ever to travel inland from the **Antarctic** coast. They did not reach the South Pole and had **scurvy** on their journey back to the ship. Shackleton was disappointed to be sent home because he was ill.

It took a lot of energy to pull the heavy sledges. The men had cocoa, **pemmican**, sugar, butter, cheese and biscuits for food.

An expedition of his own

Shackleton's next **expedition** began in 1907 on a ship called the *Nimrod*. When he arrived in **Antarctica**, there was so much ice on the sea that he and his team had trouble finding somewhere safe to land.

Shackleton sailed his ship through the ice looking for a safe place to build a hut.

There was not much room in the hut for the 15 men.

Shackleton built a hut at Cape Royds on Ross Island. He and his men spent the winter months there in warmth and safety. In Antarctica, it is dark all day and night in winter and light all the time in summer.

Journey towards the South Pole

Shackleton had brought ponies, dogs and a motor car with him to help pull the sledges across the **Antarctic** ice. After the winter passed, the men started their exploration.

The animals were glad to be on land after their long journey by ship.

The group were only 180 km (110 miles) away from the South Pole when they had to go back. They left a flag at their furthest point south.

The explorers got closer to the **South Pole** than anyone ever before, but they were running out of food and had to turn around. They nearly starved on the way back. Shackleton was **knighted** by the King when he returned to England.

Shackleton's expedition on the *Endurance*

In 1911, Roald Amundsen from Norway became the first person to reach the **South Pole**. Shackleton decided to try to become the first person to cross the whole continent of **Antarctica** instead. He set off in the ship *Endurance* in 1914.

The *Endurance* was built to be a very strong ship.

There was so much ice floating on the sea, it became hard to find a way through without damaging the ship. Soon the *Endurance* was surrounded by **sea ice** and was trapped. The men knew that the ice would not melt before the next spring. Until then, they would have to live on the ship.

The men used saws and chisels to try to keep the path through the **sea ice** open, but they could not free the ship.

Life on the ship

There was not much room for the 28 men on the small ship. The men had to clean and cook. They also had to collect ice to melt for drinking water.

It was important to keep everything clean and tidy on the crowded ship.

Shackleton checks the cracks in the **sea ice**.

The ice began to break apart when spring came. Everybody hoped that the ship would soon be able to move again. The men wanted to reach **Antarctica** and begin exploring.

The *Endurance* sinks

The ice did begin to move, but instead of releasing the *Endurance*, it began to crush her. Shackleton had to tell the men to **abandon** the ship because it was sinking.

It was a sad day when the *Endurance* broke up and began to sink.

The men made a new camp on the ice. The dogs were Canadian Huskies and did not mind the cold.

The men had to take everything with them to make a home on the ice. They slept in tents on the **sea ice** and built kennels for the dogs.

Sailing to Elephant Island

As time went on, the **sea ice** where the men were camping began to break up. Soon it was too dangerous to stay on the disappearing ice. The men had to get into three small lifeboats and try to reach Elephant Island. It took nearly a week to get there.

The boats were only about 7 metres (23 feet) long and many men got seasick.

Life was hard in the cramped, dark boats.

Elephant Island is made up of snow and ice, and rocky cliffs right down to the sea. The men turned the boats upside down and covered them with canvas sails for shelter. They had to bend over or crawl in the boats. Cooking made the sides of the boats black with soot.

The boat journey for help

Winter was approaching and Shackleton knew that no one would look for the men on Elephant Island. He decided to take a boat and try to go for help. Sailing across the Southern Ocean in a small boat was very dangerous, but it was their only chance.

Six men sailed 1300 km (800 miles) over rough seas in a little boat called the *James Caird*.

The three men walked for 36 hours without sleeping to get help.

The *James Caird* reached the island of South Georgia 17 days later. The only way to get help was to walk across the island to the people living on the other side. Crossing the mountains was very difficult, but Shackleton and two **companions** finally got there.

Rescue from Elephant Island

The 22 men on Elephant Island had to be rescued before the winter weather made it impossible. Shackleton tried three times, but the **sea ice** was too thick. Then the government of Chile lent him a ship to try one more time.

The crew of the steamship *Yelcho* and her captain Luis Pardo were happy to help.

Finally the *Yelcho* reached Elephant Island. The men there had been stranded for over four months and were nearly out of food. They were very happy when they saw a ship appear.

25

Remembering Shackleton

Shackleton seemed most at home when he was on his **expeditions**. He went to explore **Antarctica** once more on a ship called the *Quest*. Sadly, he died on the journey.

Shackleton is buried on the island of South Georgia.

This watch and **sextant** were used to **navigate** on the *James Caird*.

This is one of the boots Shackleton wore on his *Endurance* expedition.

Today, we remember Shackleton for his amazing achievements. He took his men to the icy **Antarctic** and brought them back safely. Objects and books from Shackleton's expeditions are kept in museums and libraries. Everybody can see them and learn about him.

Antarctica today

People still explore and study **Antarctica** today. Women and men from many countries go to Antarctica to find out about the ice and **climate**, and the animals that live there. This helps us to learn more about the ways **Antarctica** is changing.

Evelyn Dowdeswell, one of the authors of this book, drives a **snowcat** in Antarctica.

Map of Shackleton's *Endurance* expedition

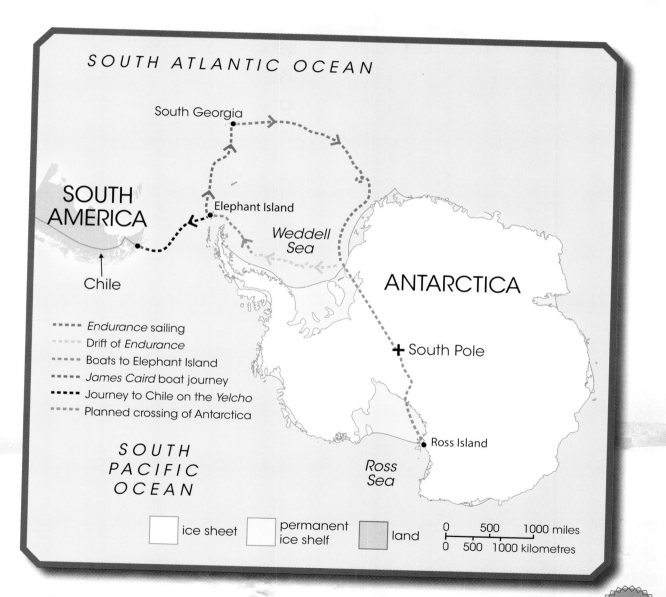

SOUTH ATLANTIC OCEAN

South Georgia

SOUTH
AMERICA

Elephant Island

*Weddell
Sea*

Chile

ANTARCTICA

+ South Pole

- - - - *Endurance* sailing
- - - - Drift of *Endurance*
- - - - Boats to Elephant Island
- - - - *James Caird* boat journey
- - - - Journey to Chile on the *Yelcho*
- - - - Planned crossing of Antarctica

SOUTH
PACIFIC
OCEAN

Ross Island

*Ross
Sea*

ice sheet
permanent
ice shelf
land

0   500   1000 miles
0   500   1000 kilometres

Sir Ernest Shackleton timeline

15 February 1874	Ernest Henry Shackleton is born.
19 April 1890	Ernest joins the **Merchant Navy** at age 16.
17 February 1901	Shackleton joins Captain Scott's *Discovery* **expedition** to **Antarctica**.
9 April 1904	Shackleton marries Emily Mary Dorman.
7 August 1907	*Nimrod* leaves Britain. This is Shackleton's first expedition to Antarctica as leader.
9 January 1909	Shackleton sets the record for reaching the furthest south.
13 December 1909	Shackleton is **knighted** by King Edward VII at Buckingham Palace.
8 August 1914	*Endurance* leaves Britain. Shackleton leads his second expedition to Antarctica.
19 January 1915	*Endurance* becomes trapped in **sea ice** and sinks 10 months later.
9–15 April 1916	Shackleton and his men get into the lifeboats and sail to Elephant Island.
24 April 1916	Shackleton and five men begin their open boat journey to South Georgia. They arrive on 10 May.
30 August 1916	Shackleton and the crew of the *Yelcho* rescue the men from Elephant Island.
17 September 1921	Shackleton starts his last trip to Antarctica aboard the *Quest*.
5 January 1922	Shackleton dies on the *Quest* in South Georgia.

Glossary

abandon leave (in this case a ship because of a problem)

Antarctic south polar region

Antarctica very cold continent located around the South Pole

climate usual weather in a place

companion someone who spends a lot of time with another person

expedition journey that is taken by a person or group of people to little known places

knighted to be given the title of "knight" by the King or Queen for doing something very good or brave

Merchant Navy group of ships and their crew that carry supplies and people during times of peace and war

navigate to find your way using maps or instruments

pemmican high energy food made of meat and fat

scurvy illness caused by lack of vitamin C

sea ice ice that forms when the surface of the sea freezes

sextant instrument that helps work out your location. It measures where the sun is at noon.

snowcat tracked vehicle that is used for travelling over snow

South Pole place that is as far south as you can go

Find out more

Books

Scott of the Antarctic, Evelyn and Julian Dowdeswell and Angela Seddon (Raintree, 2012)

The South Pole (Explorer Tales), Nancy Dickmann (Raintree, 2012)

Places to visit

The Polar Museum
Scott Polar Research Institute
University of Cambridge
Cambridge CB2 1ER
www.spri.cam.ac.uk

Index

For activity ideas and teaching notes visit: www.raintree.co.uk/content/DOWNLOAD